Mother Ghoul

Mother Ghoul

Halloween Nursery Rhymes

Collected, Spoofed, and Illustrated

by Anja Jaeger

ISBN: 978-1-7375544-2-4
Text and Character Design by Anja Jaeger
Story Design by The Purple Door Publishing
House

This book was typeset in OpenDyslexic

This collection is dedicated to all the kids at
the park that wave at me

&

To every trick-or-treater no matter your
age, you are welcome

This Book Belongs To:

Table of Contents

Table of Contents

Table of Contents

Index alphabetically by opening lines

Index alphabetically by opening lines

Index alphabetically by opening lines

Introduction & Justification for this Book

These sorts of rhymes are not just one version written by one person. This is my turn adding a twist to the classic tradition. Such rhymes and rhythms have been used for centuries to help young people learn phonics, vocabulary, counting, days of the week, and other sinister plots. It isn't like anyone reads introductions of books like this anyway so I can say anything here.

The point of children's rhymes and my spooky spoofs is not trying to take credit but rather to put my own style on classics. Some of these you might recognize and enjoy the rhythms and others might be new, not only new versions.

There are hundreds of childhood rhymes from all over the world, some of which need no help being dark and horrifying. For the most part, I left those nightmare verses alone. Instead, I have selected some that could use some fresh life (or undead-ifying) for the gothic child in all of us and the next generation of twisted kids coming up behind. Regardless, I wish you all happy nightmares.

1

Old Mother Ghoul

And old Mother Ghoul
When she wanted to roam
Would ride through the air
On a very fine broom

And old Mother Ghoul
At midnight or at noon
With a sweep of her stick,
Flew up to the moon

2

<u>Hounds</u>

At early dawn the hounds do sing
And by and by the sheep drop in
And when they bah, the hounds do say,
"Take off your things, and stay all day."

3

Vlad and Belle

Vlad and Belle went down the hill

To fetch the head of father

They came to the stream

    and started to scream

For neither could cross the water

4

Needles and Pins

Needles and pins
Needles and pins
When the doll is pricked,
     the heartache begins

5

Two Black Rats

There were two black rats
    full of dance and swagger
The one named "Cloak"
    the other "Dagger"

6

Skeleton

As I was getting up one day
My head fell off and rolled away.
But when I saw where it had gone
I picked it up and put it on.

A fellow pointed in alarm
"What has happened to your arm?"
I turned to him and kindly said
"It's fallen in the flower bed."

7

<u>Reaper Days</u>

How many days does the reaper slay
Thursday, Friday, Saturday,
Sunday, Monday, Tuesday, Wednesday,
Thursday, Friday, Saturday
The reaper wants to slay
The reaper wants to slay every day.

8

All Hallows

Monsters waiting for dinner
As the veil gets thinner

As the nights grow longer
Their hunger grows stronger

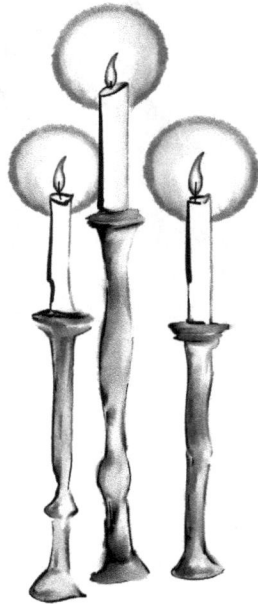

9

There Was an Old Hag

There was an old hag who lived in a shack,
Had so many onions she wanted to yak.
She chopped them up and fried them in butter
The stench filled the yard and peeled paint
off the shutters

10

Candy

If I had as much candy as I could eat
I'd never cry from the back seat
Long trips to ride, long trips to ride
I'd never cry from the back seat

11
Flicker, Flicker

Flicker, flicker, Jack o lantern
How I fear your wicked pattern
Carved into your fleshy sight
Like a demon in the night

Flicker, flicker, pumpkin light
Fearful eyes glowing bright

12

Pumpkin Face

If the North Wind does blow

And we shall have snow

Then what about poor Jack o lantern

       Poor thing, poor thing

He'll sit on the step

And his face will get wet

And a squirrel will probably eat him

       Poor thing, Poor thing

13

Five Crows

This little crow eats worms
This little crow eats nuts
This little crow drinks water
This little crow flies away
This little crow does nothing
But caws up a fuss

14

Little Blood Sucker

Little blood sucker
Sings for his supper
What will he eat?
Heart's blood and splutter!
How will he stay clean wearing white?
How will he be sated
Without a single bite?

15

Ghost Song

As I was floating along, long, long
Screeching a scary song, song, song
I haunt the woods at night, night, night
And I'll give you such a fright, fright, fright
So I went wailing along, long, long

16

<u>Zombie</u>

There was an old man
      Slept under a hill
And if he's not gone
      He lies **HERE** still

17
Scarecrow

The man in the field asked of me
"How many pumpkins grow in the sea?"
I answered him, as I thought it good
"As many skeletons grow in the wood."

18
Grave Robber

Grave robber, grave robber, have you any bones?
Yes sir, yes sir, three bags full!
One from the master, one from the wolf
One from the little boy who played with the bull

19

Three Gray Ghouls

Three gray ghouls in a black castle, shrieking
Gray were the ghouls and black was the shrieking

20
<u>Farmer</u>

Little Jack Thorne
Stood in the corn
Watching the birds feed
Dug through some weeds
Pulled out some seed
Said, what a good boy am I

21
<u>Broom</u>

Oh where oh where has my little broom gone?
Oh where, oh where could it be?
With brush cut short and handle long
Oh where, oh where could it be?

22

Crooked Cat

There was a crooked cat who walked a crooked lane
He found a crooked dog tied with a crooked chain
He broke a crooked tree so the dog could be free
And they lived together by a crooked little stream

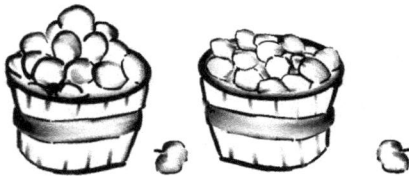

23

Apples to Sell

Red apples to sell! Red apples to sell!
I would never wail "red apples to sell!"
If I'd as much cider my thirst to quell
I would never wail "red apples to sell!"

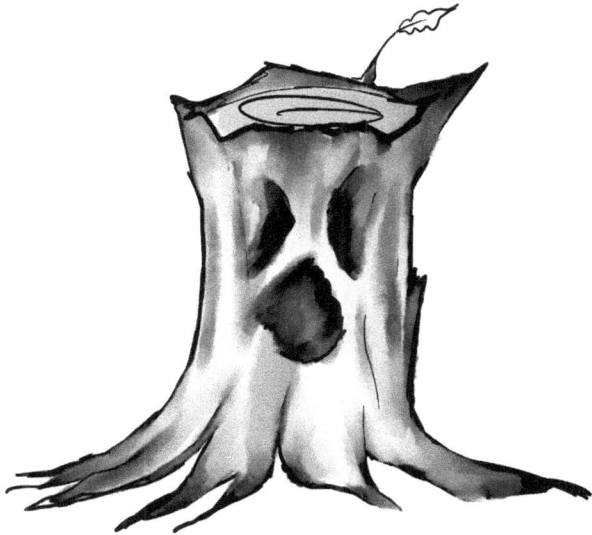

24

Three Black Bats

Three black bats
Three black bats
They all flew over the moon each night
They dropped on your face with a screeching fright
Now you're covered in scars, infected with blight
From three black bats

25

Tongue Twister Treater

Tatum trick-or-treated a ton of tricked treats
A ton of tricked treats Tatum trick-or-treated
If Tatum tricked a ton of trick-or-treated treats
Where's the ton of tricked treats Tatum trick-or-treated?

26

Fiend

The watchful fiend walked the flower fields

The more he saw the less he spoke

The less he spoke the more he heard

What was it the old fiend in the flower fields saw?

27

Lullaby

Now I put my costume away
I pray the spooky air to stay
If my candy is gone before I wake
I swear I'll make the culprit pay

28

Little Wraith, Pretty Wraith

Little wraith, pretty wraith, where do you go
Down in the swamp to and fro
Shall I go with you? No, not now
When you hear my call, I know not how

29

<u>Who</u>

I had a little owl
The prettiest ever seen
She washed the dishes
And kept the house clean
She went to the field
To fetch me a flower
And always got home
In less than an hour
She baked me my bread
And poisoned my tea
Now she's flying around
Looking like me

30

Werewolf

There was a young man called Schmitz
Once a month was troubled with fits
The cycle of moons
Threw him into a swoon
Alas! This poor young man, Schmitz

31

Three Martians

Three Martians from Mars
Went to space in three jars
And if the jars had been stronger
My song would have been longer

32

Little Miss Froglet

Little Miss Froglet
Sat on a boglet
Carving her pumpkin face
Along came a corn farmer
With husks to make armor
And took little Miss Froglet to a drier place

33

Jack Be Wicked

Jack be wicked
  Jack be cunning
Jack angered the mob
  Better start running

34

<u>Poison Potion</u>

Poison Potion in a pot
Nine days old

Poison Potion hot
Poison Potion cold
Poison Potion in a pot
Nine days old

Some like it hot
Some like it cold
Some like it in the pot
Nine days old

Spell me that without a P
And a clever witch you'll be.

35

Chicken Legs

There was an old house with chicken legs
But wherever it sat, it never laid eggs
The windows were eyes, the door was its beak
This isn't a house any child should seek

36

To Harvest

To harvest, to harvest, to pick a big gourd
Home again, home again, to build up the hoard

To harvest, to harvest, to gather some bones
Home again, home again, to the headstones

To harvest, to harvest, to slash and to cut
Run away, run away, they're harvesting what?

To harvest, to harvest, to play and have fun
Home again, home again, harvest is done!

37

Trick or Treating

Boos and ghouls come out to play
The moon is shining bright as day
Leave your slumber and leave your chores
And join your playfellows in the gore
Come with mask and come with a call
Come to share treats or don't come at all
Up the neighborhood and in the fall
A good spare pillowcase will serve us all
You find the chocolates and I'll find the sweets
And we'll have the best stash of trick or treating treats

38

Three Black Spiders

Three black spiders in a silver web, spinning,
Black were the spiders and silver was the spinning.

39
Pumpkin Head

Pumpkin Head sat on wall
Pumpkin Head had a great fall
Squish and splat, guts and stem
Pumpkin Head won't light up again

40

Little Witch, Little Witch

Little witch, little witch, where have you gone?
Gathering toads to throw in the caldron
Little witch, little witch, what's in your brew?
A potion to give your teacher the flu

41

If Wishes Were Spiders

If wishes were spiders
Beggars would spin
If dreams were your brains
Zombies would sit in my skin

42

<u>Ice, Ice</u>

Ice, ice, go away

The autumn colors are here to stay

43

What Monsters Are Made Of

What are monsters made of?
What are monsters made of?
Sludge and ashes
And pointy teeth gnashes
That's what monsters are made of

44

Mischief Night

Dark, dark
    These dogs do bark,
The monsters are coming to town;
    Some in rags
    And some with bags
And one in a plastic crown

45

Killers

Clap, clap, and stamp
Three men came to camp
And who do you think they be?
The counselor, the slayer, the undertaker
Run away, knaves all three

46

Undertaker

Undertaker, undertaker, grave ground breaker
how does your garden grow?
With victim's hearts and other spare parts
And wet-eyed mourners all in a row

47

Corvids

Of all the corvids that ever I did see
The raven is the scariest by far to me
For all day long she sits in a tree
And through my window, watches me

48

Little Black Goblin

Little black goblin
Where do you live?
Up through dark wood
Under an old bridge

49

Jack Splat

Jack Splat
Had a black cat
The cat had only one ear
But to Jack Splat
The cat was very dear

50

Mother Ghoul

Cackle, cackle, Mother Ghoul
    Flying over your wishing pool
Truly there are frights to fear
    With Halloween so near
Here are treats, take one or two
    Beware of things going...

...BOO!

Rhythm Source Guide

The choices of rhyme schemes and format of word arrangement was done to keep the spoofed version close to the original speech rhythm of the nursery rhyme people are familiar with. Below is a key of what the poems that inspired this collection of work.

1 Old Mother Goose = Old Mother Ghoul

2 At early dawn the wolf doth howl = Hounds

3 Jack and Jill = Vlad and Belle

4 When a man marries = Needles and Pins

5 There were two blackbirds = Two Black Rats

6 As I was going out one day = Skeleton

7 How many days my baby doth play = Reaper Days

8 As the days grow longer = All Hallows

9 There was an old woman = There Was an Old Hag

10 If I'd as much money as I could spend = Candy

11 Twinkle, twinkle little star = Flicker, Flicker

12 If the north wind doth blow = Pumpkin Face

13 The Five Toes = Five Crows

14 Little Tommy Tucker = Little Blood Sucker

15 As I was going along, long, long = Ghost Song

16 Pillycock, Pillycock, sat on a hill = Zombie

17 A man in the wilderness asked of me = Scarecrow

18 Bah, bah, black sheep = Grave Robber

19 Three gray spiders = Three Gray Ghouls

20 Little Jack Horner = Farmer

21 Oh where has my little dog gone = Broom

22 There was a crooked man = Crooked Cat

23 Young lambs to sell = Apples to Sell

24 Three blind mice = Three Black Bats

25 Peter Piper = Tongue Twister Treater

26 A wise old owl lived in an oak = Fiend

27 Now I lay me down to sleep = Lullaby

28 Little maid, pretty maid = Little Wraith, Pretty
    Wraith

29 I had a little hen = Who

30 There was a man at St Kitts = Werewolf

31 Three wise men of Gotham = Three Martians

32 Little Miss Muffet = Little Miss Froglet

33 Jack be Nimble = Jack Be Wicked

34 Peas Porridge = Poison Potion

35 Old woman lived in a shoe = Chicken Legs

36 To Market = To Harvest

37 Boys and girls come out to play = Trick or Treating

38 Three Gray Spiders = Three Black Spiders

39 Humpty Dumpty = Pumpkin Head

40 Little girl, little girl where have you been = Little
   Witch, Little Witch

41 If wishes were horses = If Wishes were Spiders

42 Rain, rain go away = Ice, Ice

43 What little girls/boys made of = What Monsters Are
   Made Of

44 Hark, hark the dogs do bark = Dark, Dark

45 Rub a dub, dub = Killers

46 Mary Mary quiet contrary = Undertaker

47 Of all the gay birds = Corvids

48 Little Bob Robin = Little Black Goblin

49 Jack Sprat had a cat = Jack Splat

50 Cackle, Cackle, Mother Goose = Mother Ghoul

Author's Note

Mother Ghoul all started with a zine project for Halloween to hand out with candy to trick or treaters. I don't know if anyone got a kick out of it but I could picture someone finding a random poem in their bucket, feeling eeriness and mystery stirring. Or maybe they just threw out to get to the chocolate faster. But I had fun trying to make Halloween just a little bit more weird and special, and a little less commercialized.

My education went on across different schools and languages, poetry was a solid tool used by many teachers. My grades and overall morale were always better in classes that used nonsense and play with words.

So maybe this book is just for fun to share with your kids or even your inner child. But maybe you add a poem to your traditions somewhere too. Maybe I'm still just dreaming. But that's what these poems did to me: made me dream just a little more.

Other Books By Anja Jaeger

Snow Day a lil' Boo Adventure

Beach Day a lil' Boo Adventure

Scan for more Ghoulish Books

About the Author

Anja Jaeger is a creator of spooky, supernatural stories for kids. She has a background in linguistics and a passion for folklore and uses both those skills in creating fun books for young people to enjoy with or without their grownups. Anja likes to use illustration techniques that are approachable for kids and likes to mix styles of traditional and modern in all her characters. She currently lives in an enchanted maze in the Southwest. https://www.authoranjajaeger.com/